Jill

by Rick Kristoff
illustrated by Hector Borlasca

Practice Decodable 25

McGraw Hill Education

Bothell, WA • Chicago, IL • Columbus, OH • New York, NY

MHEonline.com

Send all inquiries to:
McGraw-Hill Education
8787 Orion Place
Columbus, OH 43240

ISBN: 978-0-02-145234-7
MHID: 0-02-145234-2

Printed in China

8 9 10 11 12 DSS 27 26 25 24 23

Jill has a big job and a badge.

Jill got the big rig to stop.

There is not a traffic jam!

Scott and Dot pass Jill.

Finn Radcliff got it all on film.

A rabbit is on a bridge. See it grin!